ISBN # 0-8059-4796-5
Printed in the United States of America

First Printing

For information or to order additional books, please write:
Dorrance Publishing Co., Inc.
643 Smithfield Street
Pittsburgh, Pennsylvania 15222
U.S.A
1-800-788-7654

A

thru

Z

of

A thru Z of ANIMAL POETRY

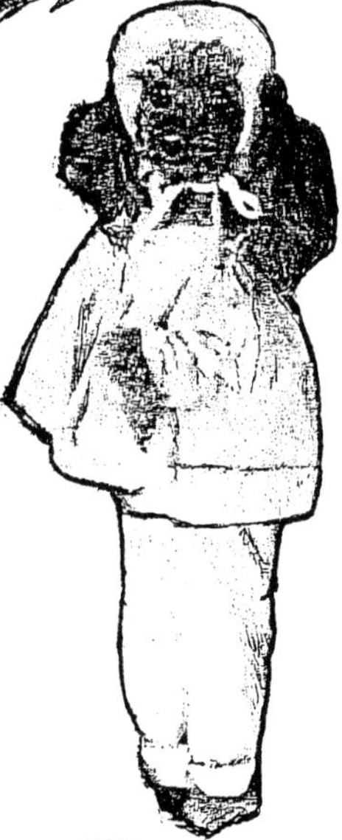

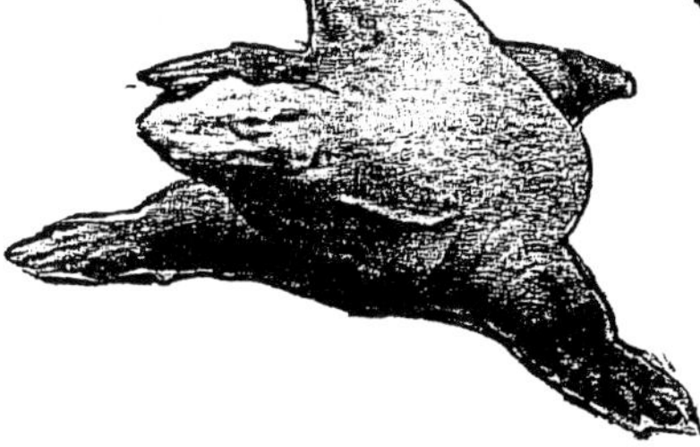

Dedication

This book is dedicated in loving memory of my son, Darryl Dennis Dean, who, like me and his brother Quinn, loved animals dearly.

All three of us absorbed and relished all the facts and stories we ever heard about animals. In our lifetimes, we were never without pets.

May this book inspire others to learn and appreciate all animals and their roles in the overall picture of this universe.

With appreciation to Mr. Johnny Carson, the most popular talk show host, for the above photo of Mr. Carson, Pandora, and me as we appeared on the "Tonight Show," March 7, 1991.

(See reference on page 31 "Parrot" poem.)

Grateful Acknowledgment

Thanks to my son, Quinn Dean, and his wife, Kathy, for the help and encouragement they gave me through the three years of hard work it took to write, paint, and photograph all the material needed to complete this book.

Their constant help and confidence in my ability was the driving force needed to compel me to put forth the time, effort, and concentration this work demanded.

Never did I hear a word of discouragement even though I am now seventy-five years old.

Quinn, by his own tenacity, in composing songs, quotes, and quips, under extreme adverse conditions, inspired me tremendously.

Thanks, Quinn and Kathy!

Contents

Sophamae
Dean Landry

Alligator

Alligators belong to the reptile class,
With snakes and lizards and such.
They are very close kin to the crocodile,
But needn't be feared as much.

The basic difference 'tween them and the crocks,
Is in the teeth and the shape of their mouths.
'Gators can grow to be sixteen feet long,
And dwell in the swamps of the south.

They feed on turtles, fish, small game,
And animals as large as a pig.
Crocks and 'gators in other parts of the world,
Though similar, don't grow quite as big.

The young are hatched from soft-shelled eggs,
That have been warmed for two months by the sun,
When a clutch of fifty or sixty have hatched,
Straight for the water they run.

'Gators are known to make a bellowing noise,
And more often in water they're found.
And though they seem very slow moving,
They can outrun a man on the ground.

< ALLIGATOR—Watercolor by Sophamae Dean Landry

Beaver

The beaver could very well be called,
The "engineer" of the animal world.
The expression "busy as a beaver" was coined,
From the way these little guys toil.

They are not as small as you might think,
Some weigh up to sixty pounds,
Including tail, might be four feet long,
As large as some hunting hounds.

They gnaw down saplings with long front teeth,
And instead of hammer and nails,
They plaster these together with mud,
Using only their broad, flat tails.

You'd think after all those years of gnawing,
Their teeth would wear away,
But, no, those teeth will continue growing,
Until their dying day.

They build their dens split-level,
Half-hidden below waterline
And here they store vegetation,
On which they will later dine.

When hunted by a predator,
Into the water they dive.
Then scurry into the upper den chamber,
Filled with air, that keeps them alive.

When danger is past, out they swim,
To complete the work of the day.
Gnawing, hauling, and plastering,
The "busy beaver's" way.

< BEAVER—Watercolor by Sophamae Dean Landry

Camel

Camels are known as "ships of the desert."
Oldest transportation in the world.
They can endure heat that is so extreme,
You might think it would make water boil.

There are two different types of camels,
And below are some distinguishing facts.
All camels belong to the family of mammals,
And all camels have humps on their backs.

The humps are the most important difference,
In the two types of camels, you see.
The Arabian, (Dromedary), has one hump,
The Bactrain has two — none have three.

Camel's feet are broad and well padded,
Protection from burning sand.
And while they make great beasts of burden,
They do not make good pets to man.

Their nostrils will close during a storm,
Keeping sand from getting in.
Their eyes have interlocking lashes,
Protection from the blistering wind.

Some camels stand seven feet at the shoulders,
And might weigh one-half ton.
When a babe is born, he could be three feet tall,
Not such a "little one."

Camels are found in Africa and Arabia,
Also, the middle east.
Leather, bones, canvas, and rope,
Can feed this hungry beast.

< CAMEL—Photo of Arabian (Dromedary) camel, Audubon Park Zoo, New Orleans, LA. Taken by Sophamae Dean Landry

Dog

Dogs are considered carnivores,
Which of course means they eat meat.
With jaws so strong and powerful,
Even bones are no great feat.

Their colors range from white to black,
With multiple hues in between.
Tan, red, gray, brown,
And "blue merle"—not often seen.

Chihuahuas being the smallest breed,
Weigh just eight pounds—so small,
With bodies well-proportioned and strong,
Standing just seven inches tall.

The rescuer, the St. Bernard,
Might weigh some two hundred pounds.
Twenty-seven inches tall at the shoulders,
Makes him the largest dog to be found.

Some dogs have traits that are rather peculiar,
Like the Basenji—the "barkless" one.
And the Chinese Crested dog has no hair,
And is easily burnt by the sun.

A companion, a protector, a helper, and actor,
A worker—without thought of pay.
A defender, a rescuer, a valued detector—
A friend 'till his dying day.

Of all the animals in this world,
(Now think of as many as you can),
Which of all these creatures do you believe
Has most endeared itself to man?

< DOG – Scarlet O'Hara – Red French Poodle.
Owner and trainer Sophamae Dean Landry

Sophamae Dean Landry

Elephant

The elephant should be called "king of the jungle,"
For no reason other than his size.
Any animal that tried to "best" an elephant,
Wouldn't be very wise.

He is the largest land animal in the world,
Weighing as much as four tons.
Calves when first born, can weigh two hundred pounds,
Much larger than most "calves" run.

There are two kinds of elephants in the world,
African and Indian or Asiatic,
The difference between these two, I would say,
Is very, very emphatic.

The Indian elephant has much smaller ears,
And a distinctly dome-shaped skull.
He is easily trained to work for man,
To haul, to push, to pull.

Think of the world without the elephant,
What a void their passing would leave.
You and I and all mankind,
Would surely sadden and grieve.

I wish the elephant lived all over the world.
But their habitats are few.
Actually, most can only be seen,
In a circus act or a zoo.

If once you've seen this magnificent giant,
He is one you'll never forget.
So go to see the elephant,
Every chance you get.

< ELEPHANT - Watercolor by Sophamae Dean Landry

Flying Squirrel

Flying squirrels belong to the rodent class,
With the mink, rat, porcupine,
Nutria, beaver, muskrat, and skunk,
And quite a few other kind.

Talk about a "babe in the woods,"
This adorable little guy,
Looks like a "babe" even when full grown,
But he really doesn't fly.

By extending four paws outward,
He is able to glide or sail.
And just as ships and planes use rudders,
He uses his broad, flat tail.

They are known to eat nuts, fruit, and berries,
Seeds, bark, and insects, too.
And they always store food for leaner days,
As many rodents do.

Considered nocturnal animals,
They feed in the dark of the night.
Sailing from tree to tree to tree,
Searching for food without light.

They measure just about seven inches long,
With fur as soft as can be.
To see them leap from a tree and glide,
Is a beautiful sight to see.

< FLYING SQUIRREL – Watercolor by Sophamae Dean Landry

Giraffe

Can you imagine what it's like to be
The tallest land animal in the world?
To reach the branches of the tallest tree,
Giraffes need not stretch or toil.

They eat nothing but fresh vegetation,
And their long necks help them survive.
When lower vegetation is depleted,
Upper branches keep them alive.

Giraffes are found in Africa,
Where plenty of food can be found.
In the part of Africa known as the "veldt"
And that covers a lot of ground.

Mom and Dad stand twenty feet tall,
And weight one thousand pounds.
When giving birth, mom stands upright
Dropping "babe" eight feet to the ground.

At birth that babe can weigh one-forty himself,
And stand as tall as a man.
For an animal to be this large at birth,
Is rather hard to understand.

There are numerous species of giraffes,
And are distinguished by color and spots,
If you look at the giraffe accompanying this poem,
You'll see lots of spots he's got!

< GIRAFFE—Audubon Park Zoo, New Orleans, LA
Photo taken by Sophamae Dean Landry

Horse

A beautiful, stately, majestic creature,
With strength, intelligence, and speed.
The young is a colt, the female, a mare,
And the high-spirited male, a steed.

A multi-faceted animal,
Can be raced, taught tricks, even plow.
And is beauty itself personified,
Unlike his bovine friend the cow.

The largest—the Belgian—stands seven feet tall,
And might weigh as much as a ton.
The Shetland Pony, only four feet high,
Is considered the smallest one.

They were introduced to the United States,
By the Spanish, many years ago.
'Till then, the American Indians,
Walked where they had to go.

The horses' role has greatly dwindled,
No longer does he trod the lanes,
Carrying men and supplies across our land,
Now it's ships, cars, buses, planes.

A female horse and male jackass
Will produce the well-known "mule."
A female jackass and a male horse,
Produce a "hinny," a genetic rule.

The oddest thing about the mule,
And the hinny, for that matter, too.
They are both infertile, can produce no young,
As their cousins, the horses do.

< HORSE—Photo of oil painting—both by Sophamae Dean Landry

Iguana
(Lizard)

The iguana belongs to the reptile class,
With alligators, snakes, and such.
And though they look just as menacing,
They needn't be feared very much.

Local—West Indies and South America,
The Galapagos, and Mexico, too,
Different locals have different kinds,
Below, I shall name just a few.

Gila Monsters and the Bearded Lizards,
Are extremely poisonous,
They are very ugly to look upon,
Avoiding these is a definite "must."

The smallest cousins to the Iguana
Are the tiny Geckos and Skinks,
They are merely two to three inches long,
And that is quite small, don't you think?

Komodo Dragons of the East Indies,
Ten feet long, might weigh three hundred pounds,
Kin to Iguanas, tiny Skinks, and Geckos,
They're the largest lizards found.

When Marine Iguanas dive into the sea,
You might think this a mere recreation,
But this is their way of sustaining life,
For they thrive on sea vegetation.

< IGUANA—(Komodo Dragon)—Audubon Park Zoo, New Orleans, LA
Photo taken by Sophamae Dean Landry

Sophamae Dean
Landry

Jackal

The jackal is considered a carnivore,
Like the dog, the wolf, the hyena.
Some folks don't know what a coward he is,
They think him to be a lot meaner.

Jackals are nocturnal animals,
And if live food is scarce, or none,
They, just like the ugly vulture,
Will feed on carrion.

They are not large nor are they small,
They weigh about thirty pounds.
In Africa, Asia, and Europe,
The carnivorous jackal is found.

There's not much more about the jackal
That I am able to tell.
One thing, though, I thought I'd add,
They give off a very bad smell.

< JACKAL – Watercolor by Sophamae Dean Landry

Saphamai
Dean
Landry

Kangaroo

If an Australian speaks of his "Joey,"
He refers to his kangaroo,
In Tasmania and Australia they are found.
And some, of course, in a zoo.

When born "Joey" fits in a teaspoon,
'Though his mom might be eighteen feet tall.
To get to his mother's "nursery pouch,"
Tiny "Joey" must crawl and crawl.

He stays there living on mother's milk,
'Till he's ten to eighteen months old.
Then out he climbs to face to world,
Reluctant, but curious and bold.

A very small head and long tapering tail,
Give this marsupial a peculiar look.
With his large hind legs and short forepaws,
He can deliver a mean left hook.

Some kangaroos weigh two hundred pounds,
Others are as small as a rabbit,
They can leap as far as twenty-five feet,
A unique survival habit.

< KANGAROO – Watercolor by Sophamae Dean Landry

Lion

The lion is called "King of the Jungle,"
And by rights has earned this name.
For he is truly the greatest of hunters,
And unequivocally rules his domain.

Lions might weigh some four hundred pounds,
And be eight feet long (with the tail),
They are golden tan to tawny brown,
And thick manes adorn the males.

The females have no manes at all,
A very significant detail,
For the mane on the lion makes the lioness seem,
Extremely dull and pale.

They live in groups that are known as "prides."
Females having just one or two cubs.
Of these, they are extremely protective,
Showing true maternal love.

To satisfy my own curiosity,
Searching, I found it was true,
Mentioned forty-eight times in the Bible,
Truly gives the lion his "just due."

For this, in itself, is significant,
Of the way man regards the lion.
"King of the Jungle"?— a suitable title,
And it suits the lion just fine!

< LION – Watercolor by Sophamae Dean Landry

Sophamae Dean
Landry

Monkey
(Ape & Gorilla)

Monkeys belong to the primate class,
And are considered very smart.
Being close to man in intelligence,
They are very easily taught.

Most monkeys are known to be prehensile,
Which means they can hang by their tails.
And they use their "fingers" as humans do.
Why, they even have finger nails!

The largest "monk" is the mountain gorilla,
Weighing five hundred pounds or more.
Walking erect, he's as tall as a man,
But "monks" generally walk on all fours.

My favorite, the pygmy marmoset,
Weighs 'bout a quarter of a pound
To me they are the cutest little guys,
Anywhere in this world to be found.

The "uakari's" looks are very weird.
With head and face—totally hairless.
His tail is a short, thick six-inch clump,
But I'm sure he couldn't care less.

In science, medicine, entertainment, too,
Monkeys are truly treasured.
Their role in man's life is so extreme,
Their worth cannot be measured.

< MONKEY (Silver Back – Mountain Gorilla)—Watercolor
by Sophamae Dean Landry

Sophamae Dean
Landry

Nutria

The nutria belongs to the rodent class,
And looks like a very large rat.
With body and tail some three feet long,
And thick fur that makes him look fat.

Classified the same as the "busy li'l beaver"
The hamster, the gerbil, and mink,
The ermine, the squirrel, the rat, and the otter
But much uglier than most, don't you think?

The nutria is considered semi-aquatic,
Is at home on land or in water.
But this rodent is not nearly as aquatic,
As his cute, playful cousin—the otter.

Not good for food, according to man,
Worth little, as animals go.
Extremely destructive to crops in the field.
Makes farmers hate him so.

The nutria is still one of God's own creations,
And he should be respected as such.
And be given humane consideration,
Even tho' he's not liked very much.

< NUTRIA – Watercolor by Sophamae Dean Landry

Sophamal
Dean
Landry

Otter

While many rodents live on land,
This cute little guy—the otter,
Just like his industrious cousin, the beaver,
Is aquatic, living mostly in water.

The fur of the otter is beautiful,
And he has a heavy undercoat.
Which keeps him warm in frigid "clime,"
And also helps keep him afloat.

Placing a clam upon his stomach,
While floating on his back,
Using a stone, he will open this clam,
By giving it whack after whack.

Otters eat birds, mussels, fish, clams,
And other food that they get from the ocean.
They eat and play and frolic about,
In a kind of perpetual motion.

To me the playful otter is,
The mermaid of the animal world.
But, some we'll have to call "mermen,"
'Cause all otters are not girls.

< OTTER—Watercolor by Sophamae Dean Landry

The city was billed twice for
some loads of trash.
Truck drivers and helpers were
sometimes weighed along with
the trash.

Parrot

The parrot is a tropical bird,
And is truly a "fowl" wonder.
Found in South America, India, Africa,
And Australia, the "country down under."

They are all considered hook-billed birds,
And can actually be taught to talk.
But without patience and proper training,
They just squawk and squawk and squawk.

There's a wide variety of parrots,
Large, small, and in between.
Colored white, purple, blue, black, gray,
Yellow, orange, pink, or green.

They live in countries with tropical climate,
Eating fruit, nuts, berries, and seeds.
Some make their nests in the side of the cliffs,
But most of them nest in trees.

To me parrots are not just "mimics."
This I know from experience.
And if I hear anyone say differently,
I'll quickly come to the parrot's defense.

Pandora, my own beloved parrot,
Is a bird that is truly unique.
Considered a yellow-headed Amazon,
She sings, laughs, cries, and speaks.

Pandora and I were on the "Tonight Show"—
With Johnny Carson in March '91.
He was then the most popular talk show host,
And we all had so much fun!

< PARROT—Photo of Pandora owner and trainer Sophamae Dean Landry

Sophamae
Dean
Landry

Quetzal

Quetzals were held sacred by the Mayans and Aztecs,
Found in Boliva and south Mexico.
They are the national emblem of Guatemala,
This keeps Quetzal's image aglow.

The Quetzal is a bird with beautiful plumage,
Belonging to the family of fowl.
With the chicken, the peacock, the duck, and the eagle,
The parrot and the "wise old owl."

His back and tail are iridescent blue-green,
A golden crest adorns his head,
A golden mantle covers part of his back,
And his stomach is a brilliant red.

One of the most beautiful birds in the world,
Measuring some three feet long.
While the Quetzal is known for his beautiful plumage,
He is not known for his beautiful song.

< QUETZAL—Watercolor by Sophamae Dean Landry

Raccoon

A nocturnal animal,
Cousin to the bear.
Raccoons are covered
With grisly gray hair.

Bandit mask on his face—
Recognized without fail.
And just as unique,
Are the rings on his tail.

They are vicious fighters,
Hunters supreme—
They forage for food,
From forest and stream.

They feed upon grain,
Birds, fruit, and honey.
They wash food before eating,
And does that look funny!

Like their cousin, the bear,
Upon hind legs they stand,
And use their forepaws,
As we use our hands.

They are good tree climbers,
And can swim very well,
They'll drown a dog twice their size,
Or, so I heard tell.

A beautiful creature,
Cunning and smart,
Their antics and playfulness,
Quickly capture one's heart.

< RACCOON—Hand carved raccoons by George Cooper
Photo by Sophamae Dean Landry

Sophamae
Dean
Landry

Shark

Sharks are found throughout the world,
And are feared by man and beast.
For they are not very particular,
On what they dine and feast.

There's a great variety of things,
On which they make their meals.
Such as man, fish, porpoise, turtles,
Plankton, whales, and seals.

Sharks have a very great range of size,
From a few inches to forty-five feet.
The "Whale Shark" being the largest—
But plankton is all "Whale Sharks" eat.

The most ferocious shark of all,
Is considered to be the Great White.
He could be compared with the Killer Whale,
Both instill fear at first sight.

"There's not a bone in his body."
Here's a fact not too commonly known—
This well applies to all kinds of sharks,
For their skeletons are cartilage—not bone.

< SHARKS—Watercolor by Sophamae Dean Landry

Turtle

The turtle is a reptile,
That carries his house on his back.
He pulls his legs and head inside,
If and when under attack.

A very slow-moving creature,
(As in the fable of the "Tortoise and the Hare.")
He just keeps right on plodding along,
Perseverance will get him there.

The turtle, tortoise, and the terrapin,
Have similar characteristics.
As for size, weight, and general appearance,
Here are just a few statistics.

Certain species, when they are fully grown,
Four to seven inches they run.
While others grow to twelve feet long,
Weighing a quarter of a ton.

Most kinds of turtles are very docile.
You will seldom see them fight.
But the "Logger Head" and the "Snapper"
Can deliver a very mean bite.

< TURTLE—Audubon Park Zoo, New Orleans, LA
Photo taken by Sophamae Dean Landry

Sophanee Dean
Landry

Uakari

The Uakari is a primate or monkey,
And though his name begins with a "U"
The proper pronunciation is "Wakari."
Why "Wakari"? I haven't a clue.

In some ways he's very much like his cousins,
In other ways he really is not.
Where Uakari features are concerned,
He differs quite a lot.

They do not have prehensile tails,
Instead a broad, six-inch clump.
But he's very active in the tops of trees,
Leaping twenty feet at a jump.

Like other primates in their class,
They use their "fingers" as men do.
Their coloring is white, or chestnut brown,
And some have a reddish hue.

You might consider "Uakari" ugly,
But I am sure his relatives don't care.
What is most odd looking about him is
His head and face have no hair.

He is as bald as any "Q" ball,
And looks like a little old man.
But to all the other Uakari, I am sure,
His appearance is simply grand.

< UAKARI—Watercolor by Sophamae Dean Landry

Sophamae
Dean
Landry

Vulture

In my mind, the vulture is
The ugliest bird you can find.
Take a look at this bird, and you will see,
That I'm not just being unkind.

The vulture has a long, skinny neck,
A head with no feathers at all.
With legs and body long and lean,
When standing he seems rather tall.

He will not hunt or kill his food,
When others eat then turn away,
Mr. Vulture moves in and consumes what's left,
And that is his meal for the day.

The vulture's a beautiful sight to see,
While soaring high overhead.
But investigate the spot below,
And you're bound to find something dead.

< VULTURE—Watercolor by Sophamae Dean Landry

Sophamae
Dean
Landry

Whale

Whales are found all over the world,
From the southern most part to the North Pole.
They breathe through holes in the top of their heads,
Through what is commonly called a "blowhole."

Whales do not have gills as all true fish do,
But lungs, just as you and I.
After diving, they must resurface for air,
Without which, they would surely die.

They are the largest animals in the world,
Larger than were most dinosaurs.
One hundred feet long and weighing five tons,
They outsize the elephant, by far.

Hunting for food, whales can stay submerged,
For as long as maybe an hour.
That depends on the size of the whale, of course,
For the larger ones have more lung power.

Hunted until they were doomed to extinction.
(And that was so very sad.)
For in oil, blubber, bones, ambergris,
There was a lot wealth to be had.

The whale did provide food for man,
But to kill whales to make some cosmetics?
To endanger this magnificent animal,
Was truly very pathetic.

The lack of demand for those by-products,
Was a true blessing for the whale.
Now we need not fear he'll become extinct,
The happy end of a whale of a tale.

< WHALE—Watercolor by Sophamae Dean Landry

Sophamae Dean
Landry

Xenopus

The Xenopus is a small clawed frog,
Though the name begins with and "x,"
The "x," you see, is pronounced like a "z."
So "Zenopus" is considered correct.

An amphibian found in Africa,
Just about five inches long.
If you think his claws are of no use,
You are very, very wrong.

When threatened by a predator,
Into the water they dive,
And clouding the water by kicking up mud,
These claws help to keep them alive.

This is his one and only defense,
No poison or powerful jaws,
So the xenopus manages to stay alive,
By kicking up mud with his claws.

< XENOPUS—Watercolor by Sophamae Dean Landry

Sophamae
Dean
Landry

Yak

Yaks are found in the high country
Of the Himalayas and Tibet.
Some yaks are very domesticated,
As beasts of burden, not as pets.

The yak is a kin to the wild oxen,
Weighing some twelve hundred pounds.
Long silky hair hangs from their sides—
So long it touches the ground.

The silky hair, used for clothes and blankets,
Make the yak a vital resource,
And even more important is the meat and milk,
For sustaining life, of course.

Considering the size and the weight of the yak,
They are agile climbers, indeed.
Mountains and glaciers are no obstacles,
They can even swim, when there's need.

< YAK—Watercolor by Sophamae Dean Landry

Zebra

Zebras belong to the equine class
With the jackass, the donkey, the horse,
The mule, and, oh yes, the burro,
All kin to the horse, of course.

The zebra is smaller than the horse,
Some four and a half feet tall.
They are stubborn, ill tempered, and very mean.
Domesticate them? Not at all!

Zebras are the only horse-like creatures,
With stripes which help keep them alive.
In the shade these stripes blend in to form
A wonderful camouflage.

Do you think all zebra's stripes are alike?
Well, this is more than a hint.
The zebras' stripes are as individual
As a human's fingerprint.

Observing the zebra with all of the stripes,
On his head, his legs, his back,
It is hard to determine if zebra stripes
Are black on white or white on black.

< ZEBRA—Audubon Park Zoo, New Orleans, LA
Photo taken by Sophamae Dean Landry